SEASHORE

HANNAH CAO

SEASHORE

Cover photo copyright © Public Domain via Unsplash

Cover design: Hannah Cao

Illustrations: Ngoc Anh Phan

ISBN: 9798613833849

www.hannahcao.co.uk

My lover & my rocks,

may you feel the breeze of the sea within these pages

CONTENTS

ACKNOWLEDGMENTS
ABOUT THE WRITER

The wearer of warmth and abundance is a different one for everybody. Perhaps a location, a person, a song. For me, that's Brick Lane Bookshop. It's reading *Lolita* in Regent's Park with sunglasses on. Sitting in an anonymous pool of stairs at Piccadilly Circus. Surrounded by tourists from Shanghai and buskers singing Beatles songs only a dozen times. My face buried under his arm in his lap. The turquoise silhouette of Nha Trang Beach in my home country Vietnam, or on top of the roof of my late grandmother's house in the village of Hà Nội.

Some of us are lucky enough to find comfort in our own home, within our very own bones. To feel that lucky, I wrote this book. To shed the shame, bury the past, reflect on darling memories and embrace the love I feel and receive today. To never forget. To forgive, forgive, forgive.

I wrote and thought, erased and tried, because sometimes being a writer hurts. I wrote these passages in the very heat of the moment. On the tube at five in the morning still hungover from tequila shots and berry cider. Before the sun rose to the sky. I wrote these when I was distracted with work, after rocky therapy sessions. I wrote these gone on a holiday. I wrote these with him sleeping inches away from me and my heart beating in my face.

And I wrote these as I fell out of my frame in my dimly lit bedroom at night, a wine glass on the nightstand in my messy, tiny student apartment.

At times it's as though the rising sun is smiling with me, and for a moment the horizon seems so wide. Other times, the water is curling over me like a consoling blanket as I cry. This collection explores that gentle rise and fall. The ocean, too, is a restless heart.

Kisses from the sea,
Hannah

"[…] I went right
back the next day, but in a t-shirt
and didn't try to be pretty, just
swam like something ordinary,
something worthy of the sea."

– Ada Limón

SEASHORE

LONDONER

QUIET PARTY

See out citywide, don't know what we see
Cars moving collaterally,
Blackbirds calling from up the hill

Climb pink stairs to Frank's rooftop bar
Look out over at downtown
Sirens blasting, hear it from afar,
so loud, so noisy
We're right here, so quiet, so sweet

The sky looks like a party,
the backstreet like a date
Eat up these moments, that's what they say

Meet me for a cider on top of Primrose Hill

Come on over on every weekday
Stay up 'til morning playing pretend
Talking, drinking, sharing cigars,
mending whatever is left to mend
This station's too rowdy to remain insignificant

Fixing a heart with your own that is broken
Holding hands where the touch feels frail

The way I feel right now,
is it the moon? Is it the company?
I don't know if that's a star or a satellite rocket
Never witnessed white-hot fireballs, in fact,
never taken a moment to stop and stare
Then I wonder why there's none in the sky

Everything's gonna be okay, I promise

Everything's gonna turn out the way
everything's supposed to

We've not enough time or money
to do what we want (if we knew)
We've too much booze to keep our roots
in the ground (if we had any)
Hear you cackling at the pub,
cheeks of crimson, head over heels falling in love
(Or are you just laughing at me?)

Do I stay or go,
I never really know
There's red lipstick
stains
on coffee cups

I could have another life but I have mine
and in the midst of Soho's Roxy pivot,
we are fine

LIVERPOOL STREET

There are around fifteen people
and how
can one be so socially deprived to be chatting
with the driver throughout the whole ride?
The semi-packed coach from Stansted Airport takes
about forty-five minutes to Liverpool Street
It took a little longer this time
Missed the last train going North that night
Six months worth of clothing
in two small luggages, one backpack
Broken heel on one shoe,
clack, clack, clack, clack… The sound of
my old life migrating with me to the new,
really might not be coming back this time

Called my best friend 'cause she was still awake,
then texted Mum, letting her know I'm OK
Turned off the lights, watched the curtains sway
while the window's closed
The bed: inconsolably huge for a soul without direction, someone
so lost, still floating,
my body like my mind

Liverpool Street, starting point of a life (my life)
Shaken up Reality (how I once knew it)
So mundane, so plain (that was all)
Now shimmering, so new (upside down)
A dream feeling real,
a reality that feels like a dream

Start off with a title page
for a story book of places and people
I knew I could call mine

(At least for a while)

What kind of leap it was to peek
down on the city from my lonely hotel room
and pray I wouldn't crash

To realise just how much space it means to say "the world"
Endless – didn't even know it
Right underneath my nose – couldn't even touch it

I am somewhere there and maybe
it doesn't matter much
but the moment matters to me

I wonder if everyone in this city gets to experience this,
has their breath sucked away
and is fuelled, by packed streets,
with new oxygen to live by

Even though I wept in qualm
of myself and what was to come,
Liverpool Street looked a lot
different in the morning

FLAT SOUND

Maybe it was the fact I set the scene of getting on this ship
knowing I am never going to see these faces again

I must say it's a refreshing, somewhat reassuring
but atrocious thought, all around
Don't like being robbed of what I've found
Don't like losing sight of where I stood but
some moments need drenching to stay good

I wonder what you're doing
and whether you're wondering the same thing about me
I remember you prefer thrifting but are you still shopping at that
boutique?
Are you still friends with the girl who led you on?
Did you confront that guy who pressured you or did you let it
slide?
What about the girl you kissed without saying goodnight?
Does her boyfriend know?
Have you opened your café?
Did your old Chantilly cat come through your door at home and
purr?
What about your journal you lost in Spitalfields Market?
I believe it was around this time
as I walked through the dry fields
of Harrow-on-the-Hill in June
when I stopped chasing the shadows

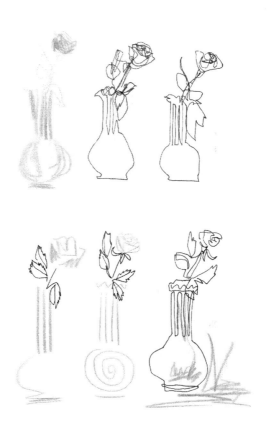

THIS CITY KNOWS

This city doesn't care
yet it knows who you are
Doesn't mind where you're from,
if you wake in the morning with scars across your shoulders
Have you ever been to place
just because it was a place
and you deserved to be there?

This city knows you're lonely,
keeps everybody in despair,
desperate for connection, relation
until you become that character
entering, staying, bleeding, leaving
and after all of that, still believing

No one in this city knows just
what exactly they are doing
what they're feeling or what
they're supposed to be standing up for
They pick up matches and set themselves on fire

In this city it's OK if you
don't know where you belong or
don't know where the fuck you stand
East or West or South or North
or with anybody
or constantly moving back and forth
from one job to another
It doesn't matter because nothing matters right now
and absolutely nothing's for certain

Maybe we don't want it to be
This city already knows, you see

Somewhat dangerous, this town,
where time stands still, stories of prosperity bask in the sunlight
And we sense failure sitting in our guts
like fleeting visitors still

Yet it doesn't matter on the elevator that's simply going up
Where the sky is bright at night
because there is no limit
And that in itself makes you feel so damn restricted
Don't you get it?

If you wanna feel special, this is not the place
If you wanna get found, this is not the time,
You'll feel it in the way they kiss
For some this hell is bliss
I truly miss it

And it's not the fault of this city
Because it knows, you see

So many people, but don't expect to be bewitched
So much movement, but don't expect to be fast
This city *is* the constant state of flux
Everything is overwhelming, if you see it that way,
but you're never trapped
You roll up next morning to make last night wash past

Spilled coffee on the sidewalk,
scarf stuck in between seats,
the bus takes the corner

And suddenly you see him,
you see Thames with his hopeful
eyes in the mimicked sky

Listen closely, love
This city is trying to speak to you, love

The magic here consists of feeling like everyone
and no one at all
Sometimes you're part of it, sometimes you'd rather be gone,
have it swallow you up in its grey wet pavement
You disappear for a bit and life's already moved on
This city knows it's always darkest before dawn

POUNDS

You don't want to pay for the bus fair
even though it's only one pound fifty
It's not a lot
but stuff adds up in this city
And you're starving for a few days to get by

You're shedding some pounds off your stomach
so what could be the harm?

You isolate yourself in your rectangle box
Your bed is also a dinner table and working desk
You save up what you can
to experience what everyone else does
You'd rather live in misery than miss out
and you're always out and about

Walking down Oxford Street in haste to feel the
city's breath on your cheeks
Hear it whisper lovely nothings, seduce you
to get on your knees
All the while you try not to notice how light
the purse in your pocket feels

It's a common thing here to drown
Some say they've never felt more down
You sure had your moments
But you're not leaving this town

PLEASE QUIT SMOKING

You never stopped walking on the escalator
no matter how far behind I stood
And you never waited for the next tube in four minutes
You always had to come for the same shift

You caught up with me when I refused to follow,
even in our office space

We watched movies in expensive theatres
and you treated me to Japanese dessert
It was good in Chinatown, shite anywhere else
You always had smoke puffing through your lips
except for when we were kissing

Always bought new cigarettes
in the tiny shop across the street
And you never ate chicken
Still kissed me when I did

You'd play basketball with the boys in the fields
when I lay at home and cried
I thought it's just not your job to be mine
all the damn time

(Maybe you wanted to be
Maybe I pushed you away)

I felt differently about you in a couple of weeks' time
after overthinking about you and I for a while

Keith from the Costa shop convinced me
to let go if it feels wrong, even when I told him
you did everything right

He knew what I needed and what I wanted
and that those things were not with you by my side
.

You insisted we'd spend the day together regardless,
as friends, makes sense

You brought me home, got out a last cigarette from the box
from the back of your trousers before you tossed the
paper in the next bin

You can't do it, you said. You can't be friends with me,
you can't bear how it feels when I don't lay my head
on your shoulder on the Jubilee line or when your hand is not
wrapped around mine in Park Lane

We apologised for not being for each other
and thanked each other for trying
that in grey London weathers, we attempted to be
each others' lightning

The last text I ever sent was to please quit smoking
but I was sure enough Trafalgar Square heard you puffing

NEVER MORE THAN FRIENDS

We sat by the lake drained by the river streams
and watched no soul in particular
because there was no one in sight
I stumbled in a yellow dress and fell on my elbow right in front
of you
and you didn't laugh

Blood oozed from my sides as you held me
You were always so hesitant as if my limbs were gleaming
A dozen corners later you hurried across the store looking for
bandaids, then splashed the water you bought all over me to put
them on
You got me ice cream with a smile of a child

It melted away in the sultriness of tangerine days
before I could even put my lips on it
Were you imagining things?

We often watch what's around like a movie
instead of being actors and actresses in it
and we've always wanted to become its writers

We met that one night at the pub,
you were with your mates and I was with mine
We spent hours walking through the fields
reassuring each other that things would be fine
as though we'd known so much about each other
or what was going on

I am sure that we didn't
In reality we were still strangers
but we also didn't mind

Our glances were seldom intense
We were never more than friends
but we knew we were just playing pretend
in the end

CATCHING TRAINS

There are worse things
than being stuck between strangers
standing right beneath their armpit
with the height of five feet

Soaked at the station on blazing days,
running to catch the train,
twisting an ankle, getting to the office
with nothing but mush in your brain

Money is motivation, sir
Paperwork you don't remember giving me?
Already in motion, sir
Life itself trying to keep up with the pace
in this town of woe I don't even feel like myself

What is that goddamn place we are constantly running to or
getting away from?
I swear to God I hear the earth cry underneath our shoes as we
stomp
Truth be told, all our fates start from crumbs and they've been
combed

And I'd never do these things if I hadn't met you
I would've never dared to chase him,
given him my number,
hadn't I wanted to be more like you

And I'm afraid of fire and spiders and heights and death and
neglect
I'm afraid of needles and the dark and abandoning my nest
and terrified of rejection and drowning
but none of that in London

RUNAWAY

In Soho your green eyes looked surprisingly full
across from me in that packed Thai restaurant
I felt the corners of your mouth pull
We agreed we wouldn't call it a date
I'm leaving London in a couple of days

Posed a question you must've had on your mind all day
"When exactly are we going to run away?"

I don't know what to say,
I'm in London and I already ran away

FOR THE LOVE OF A DAUGHTER

CRIMSON CRAYON

I am ten years old and in fourth grade
when my desk has crimson crayon
manifested on its surface
I hadn't used crayon in a year
and forgotten where I'd put it

My palms are pushed flat against the hardwood
until my fingers turn pale, as if the more stiff
my hands feel, the less damage they will make in my room

I'm not praying, not verbally,
I don't know what to pray for
I am simply hoping for the best

Ba will punish me if I make a mess again
He will ask why my cheeks are red and puffy
and wet and my expression so bitter, so ugly
Do I remind him of Ma when I am looking this way?
One time she stood before him with her head held high in a
marine blue dotted dress and I'd heard him tell her that
I think she just wanted to be held then

I found solace in sitting without saying a word;
at this young age I would rather be dead
It's what he taught me to do best

On Wednesday after school I tried to run away from home with
my baby sister; she was only three
Like a fool I got punished for being reckless,
got scolded for being selfish, *I wasn't raised that way*
I also disappointed Ma that time
I swore to her it wasn't her but Ba I wanted to leave behind

That night I pray to the universe, the stars,
the half-moon glooming above
I wonder if my small voice is desperate enough to reach them
I pray that you sleep soundly, Ma
That my little baby sister won't wake up from his voice banging
from inside his mouth,
trap of nonsense falling out
That you'd drown out his yelling
echoing down the hallway of our second floor apartment in this
crappy town we must call home or we won't have one

He doesn't have to call you by names
when you can already hear what he thinks by his tone
I catch the same pronunciation slipping from my innocent
tongue here and there
and I feel ashamed
I don't even understand it but I'm learning the slang he speaks in
Vietnamese
Tại sao chúng ta ở đây? Why can't we just leave?

Because I'm too young to understand
You've accepted your prisoner's fate
as karma and you care more about us than yourself
Sometimes I wish that wasn't the case

I feel like my ears are pounding every time he speaks, like an
overly charged heart in a baby bird's chest
I'm too young to understand what this means

Maybe that's the way you think: It's better if my daughter
doesn't know, it's better to play pretend
Children grow up healthier with both their parents in the end
But maybe children aren't that dull and maybe a child like me
doesn't want you to bend
You don't think I'll remember when I'm older

until I tell you about it later

I'm not praying, not verbally,
I don't know what to pray for
I am simply hoping for the best

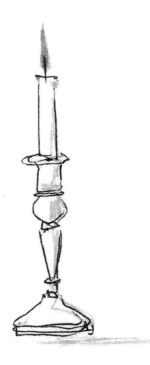

SIXTEEN

Cat's in the sack now,
won't you tell me now?
Fourteen, fifteen, sixteen,
I'd say it's time to come clean

Ma, what's the truth?
Is it him or you?
You can pull my loose tooth
but can't see this through?

You're smiling a grimace, barely laughing,
and when you do it's in odd timing
I know what it looks like,
yeah, I mean your real smile
And to be honest, I haven't seen it in a while
You're fooling me,
please sit
I think Ba and you might have to split,
It would be better, wouldn't it?
Is it not the way you see it?

Just like that time by the bay,
can we just sit by ourselves and chat?
Ma, are you okay?
Why do you cry when I ask that?

BACKYARD

We used to play in the high grass in the backyard
and every older lady with their laundry basket was our
grandmother

I learned to love being in the water in a pool set up right there
on dry tares, coloured baby blue in the shadow of dusk
and I almost drowned in the swimming hall in fifth grade
I was too embarrassed to admit I was a beginner to my
classmates

Instead I followed them when they went ahead to dive
That was the first time I got scared for my life

It didn't stop me from swimming again, somehow I'd made it a
mission to turn water into a safe space, turn its salt into a vein of
mine
I couldn't stand the world working against me,
I wished it would move beside me like a friend

And I swam again
to get over that fear and taught my sister how to turn
the tides into a mattress, a smooth hug

Something that felt so embracing couldn't be of harm
I teach myself, yet until now I am afraid to drown

(I jump and hope I don't slip too deep)

I guess growing up took my breath away
I guess growing up just feels this way
You get spat out and swallowed up at the same time
And somehow you don't mind

Every heart you learn to know better changes
as the seasons and the spring birds like to tell
the story of the ebb and the tide always meeting in the middle
with their limbs in a song to intertwine

One day your head reaches beyond the surface facing the sunrise
and the wind dries the dirt on your skin against the sun
And
you're at your old home in the same backyard
And
you're the only one who feels the same

HIS LITTLE GIRL

I do not feel like his little girl
 even though he made me
I did not feel protected
even when he held me
I never wanted him to come to Parent Day to school

I didn't ask him to drive me there
Not even back home in the afternoon
But he insisted to

Maybe I'd skip school
Be a naughty girl
Maybe I'd kiss boys
And not just one or two
or all of my guy friends
And he got mad at me whenever I rolled my eyes at him in the backseat

How can you trust someone that shares your blood
but you barely know at all?
How can he know I'm only good for trouble
when he's never praised the moments I stood tall?

I do not wonder what made him this way anymore,
I cannot judge because I know nothing of him,
Not his history, not what he feels
just like my mother when she met him
and still can't tell who he is
after all these years

Now it's midnight in your timezone
You say you love me on the phone
for I am so far away

What the hell do I even say?
I don't even know if your new family lives in a house or a flat
And you don't seem to think there's something utterly absurd
about that

I'm still your little girl, you say
Actually I haven't been for a while
But I'd say I still turned out okay

SNOW WHITE

The Scholz family lived across from us in the hallway
and I would call them my grandparents without
knowing their full names or being able to read the
psychologist's ineligible handwriting on their bell's label

Ma was pregnant with my baby sister at the hospital
and I missed her on the left side of the bed beside me,
my arms usually hooked with hers like the braids she
effortlessly bound in my hair in the morning

The new digital alarm clock Ba got came with a display
which hit the ceiling with purple digits like lightning daggers
invisible in the shadow, shooting through dream dust
It was eleven o'clock, just before midnight, and the right
side of the bed was cold when I expected to feel Ba's back
as I extended my arm from below the blankets with my eyes
closed

I would've fallen back asleep if he had been there but I was
on my own and I have never been on my own at night before
In the silence where I sat underneath our warm sheets I began
trembling, and I found being alone scary, not being able to see

I turned on all the lights as quickly as I could and sprinted
between rooms, abandoned and helpless with one sock, a pyjama
top with long sleeves hanging over my hands and a doll, that
meant nothing to me with my parents beside me, in my armpit

I was afraid of the dark, yet I kept crawling in it expecting to find
Ba somewhere; he was possibly just cooking, getting a midnight
snack, snuck into the living room to watch the last episode of a
series he had started, folding laundry, checking on the bills... all
of that but he would surely not abandon me

I don't know what made the feeling sink into my stomach
but I felt unsafe at home under the sickle moon and the
laundry hung cold out on the line in the living room

In my haste I ran outside into the deep winter's
cold to look for his car which was gone, too
I forgot the door would shut itself close behind
me, then I stood there and couldn't ring my way
back home

It was the Scholz couple from next door that heard
me bawl by their window and when I saw their lights
come on I rang their bell
It was late now but how late I couldn't tell
I was looking for an eternity

"What do we do with this one?" Lucia asked her
husband as they wrapped me in a blanket and sat
down beside me on their couch as if this had been
something we've always done
For a moment I believed it because when Stephan
Scholz looked down at me and adjusted my doll to
sit up next to me and asked "Do you want to
watch Snow White?" I let out a sigh of relief and
nodded my head

They watched the movie on the TV on cassette with
me until Ba came back and I didn't question why or where
he'd gone, I didn't want to go back home
because I guess ever since I feared being alone
and I feared not everyone would be like the Scholz Family
and not everyone would stay up so I wouldn't be on my own

SHOEBOX

The shoebox on top of Ma's tall bedroom closet had dust sitting on its lid like a film of ancient grains of sand in the soles of summer sandals. It smeared thickly on her fingertips the moment she opened it. The last time I saw Ma look through its contents, her chest was stiff and shoulders hanging. Her hands were hovering nervously and I watched the dust dance in the light of a sunset ray hanging in the room. At first she had her back turned to me, her focus distant and fixed, as if I wasn't there. I'd never seen her acting odd but somehow I knew she wasn't thinking clear. Or maybe she did. I don't know how I knew that she was crying before she even turned to me. I had to come around the sofa to take a look and she had opened a photo book on her lap.

It sat on her like a wet piece of paper ripped in the middle of the page. She didn't make an attempt to hide her sorrow, or the book with the pile of pictures we took. Of her, my baby sister and me and parts that were missing. Parts that showed Ba but she had cut him away. *He had done something terribly wrong* was my first thought and I hated that I already knew I was right. A child already knew disappointment through the smell of their parents' skin hugging them, how more broken can hearts be born?

I think even then at 6 years old I felt it in my chest that everything was about to change. An odd feeling sat in the pit of my stomach as I looked at those photos knowing Ba had been in them but now wasn't anymore. I didn't know what it meant. It didn't feel right but Ma never did anything that wasn't right. So I thought this was how things were going to be.

That's when she told me that Ba will come home at seven, as he does every day after work, so absolutely nothing changes and I'll put on the rice cooker for dinner the way she taught me how.

Ma looked at me smiling and put the pictures and the parts severed back in the shoebox. It lay right there on our living room's glass-topped table until Ba came home. He didn't look in it or cared for what was inside.

DINING TABLE

You always loved falling asleep to thunderstorms
and downpour while they fought
You preferred the calm approach of the sky weeping to
the thump of sobs coming from your pillowcase
The roaring reminded you too much of your father
when he started harsh arguments by the dining table,
you retreating to your room leaving a full plate
of your mother's cooking behind

He'd come into your room more times than you could count to
apologise,
but you were purely listening to the drizzle whisper
little truths into your ear

Said that this will happen again
And an apology is no promise
And his promise is no promise that he'd keep

The rain would tell stories about April showers
and midsummer rumbles that would drown out the voice
of the monster living on the other bed

Count lessons that are false and imprinted in your mind anyway,
like drops on your white coiffure in the springtime
You and the rain made a promise to sway and waltz
whenever you'd cross paths
None of you knew that when you dance in wet clay,
his limbs are flailing about
None of you realised not everyone else standing nearby
will be pleased to find grey speckles on their trousers

FOREST DOWN HERE

Ba, I am not her
And neither is Ma
Ma, I don't think I'm the daughter you think I am
or the type of daughter you hoped I'd be
Little sister, I need some therapy and you're too young to understand
You say I laugh so much I'm pretty
But every meal I eat tastes bland
Do you not see how my knees are never still?
Each night I sit by the windowsill talking with the moon
until I get sick
I would like some rehab, some therapy
I would like some fucking help
I am not this,
not used to this,
used to be positive
used to have perspective
How do I change back?
Used to be so different,
now it's hard to keep track
I am running in circles in an attempt to get away
From time to time I turn around and think I'd rather stay
From place one to place two, till the next comes around
How long can I keep it up before I hit the ground?

DEAD TO ME

Sometimes I fantasise about telling people you are dead
Even though I know I don't actually mean for it to be true
It's how disappointed I have become that it feels like you are, too

And I don't really want you back
And I don't really want you here
I don't admit I miss you
Like you were meant to disappear

Why do you still call on my birthday?

Sometimes I forget we used to have a car
You drove us to our first vacation to the Baltic Sea
Even when you had to drive back home alone for work
And the journey was pretty far

And I really wanted you to stay
And I really wanted you there

Did you work hard?

Sometimes I forget how long it's been since I've seen your ageing
face
I don't even know a single story from your past
And I wonder if you ever read me stories before bed
It's hard to imagine you being dead

What goes through your mind at night?

I hope your kids grow up well
And you hug them in the moonlight
That you have no reason to yell
or to leave them for life in a fight

TO BUILD A HOME

Neat set up rows of pillows on flower beddings
sprawled on clean white bed sheets
A child's face bruised in innocence,
where skin and bandaid meet

All for my safe haven,
you always made me laugh
All words were forgiven
The sun rose through each cloud

All you did I didn't know of,
it pains to hear your cries
when you tell me stories of the past
that seems blown up in lies

A tale of Ms Unfortunate,
a song of flames goes by
A sob-filled hug in long late hours
could make the devil cry

I write this to whisper thank you
and beg for your forgiveness,
for all the times I nodded
to words that I resisted
And for being this reckless

I write this to embrace you
Hoping that could heal the pain
and maybe express in actions
for words I cannot say

GRIEF

"The tide goes slowly and it can't be stopped"
You gave me *Little Women* to read growing up
never expecting our last visit would be a grace cup,
for you to remind me of it

It sort of felt like my world tipped over and wilted
by the edges when the lighthouse lost sight of you
when the shore let you sleep on it
Stephan, I don't think you knew just how much I wanted
you to walk me down the aisle

I always thought you'd still make it to the day I marry
the love of my life the way you did
and I would smile with you there and you would tell me
how proud I've made you as if I was your own
Ich hab' dich lieb / I love you
End of every visit
Last to my letter

For the rest of my days I'll take this loss for a lesson
to never hide my affection
because now I'm not sure if you knew
and I really hope you do

You always said you wanted to leave
before your wife does
I see it in her eyes, the way she cries
Was it better without a goodbye?

I refuse to believe I was born to grieve

Yet the heavens on that day looked bright and deep,
dazzling overhead, and the Beatles played as we lay you down

Yesterday, all my troubles...

We buried a body that reminds us of you
in the blue yonder
The birds have since pulled blankets up to your chin
every night

Cleaned your face every morning
and sometimes we do things
simply because you would do them

And we gather to sing together
Yesterday...

UNBORN

I would've been a brother, a sister,
a shelter, a keeper,
a dashboard for forgiveness,
a dumpster for emotions

If it were for me,
if I had existed,
Would she be they way she is?
Would she cry as much as she does?
Would she be laughing more, loving more deeply?
Would words pour from her fingers just the same?
Would she trust as little?

She wishes I was there,
take some of her burden
But she wouldn't have learnt to draw strength from her own
breath

She is the sister, a shelter,
a promise keeper
A pinboard of emotions,
a hoarder for forgiveness
Slashed by past mistakes that were never hers to make
and flaws that were never hers to carry

She is rain hoping for shelter
She is the running breeze

THE DEEP SEA

DUST STORM

I've seen the moon disappear
behind colossal horizons
I've seen pebbles crumble
on concrete
I've seen my hands quiver
beneath gentle touch

I've seen the pouring rain and a thunder cyclone
and the shadows burn
Tears staining the carpet like a spilled Sauvignon
in the cadence of the midnight hours

I am an unstable dust storm,
a volcano ready to explode
and the magma might burn just
well beyond what my body knows,
what it holds
What would it leave behind?

Please drown my emotions
Dissolve them from my bones
No matter where they fall I hope they'll fit
In heavenly lakes, blue and sunlit
White loaf of nothing
in an ashy black pit

WHITE NOISE

Your excuse has always been that screaming in your head you can't escape until you do what it says / You call it your gut because that seems just right, and sometimes that's enough / You cannot say what you think, don't you see? / Your gut is not your anxiety / Don't go and get it confused

Your emotions are a trap and you are a honey bee / Your gut bears a different name / It carries feathers on its back and not a mouth big enough to yell / Your gut is not a home / even though it's built as one

It's the gentle whispers humming songs of what is truly good for you / Can you pretend to ignore what is screaming in your head at you / even louder the more fearful you get? / Can you escape it?

If you listen closely / The loudness feeds off the panic you provide its fingers / It will grasp onto them if you're not careful enough

I get that you often forget to look out for yourself / Follow the whisper, honey / Where there is wailing and crying there is always a whisper / Somewhere underneath the Red you'll find it / It comes in peace and looks at you with love / Now go follow it / Let the noise wash away / Turn the Red into Blue / Until the swirls and whirls fade

LOOSE THREAD

I don't like to talk about what hurts,
it might make me feel like it's all there is,
I don't want to believe that,
my mind already does

I don't like to brag about the good things,
I'm afraid they'll up and leave
before I've even had the chance to touch them
I don't want to believe that they will,
my mind already does

People love to say I love too much
Blame it on my emotions, how I like to be touched
I don't want to believe I give up too much,
my mind already does

CIRCLE

Train on a track
Constantly moving somewhere
Turns out, after years, it's been
going 'round and 'round
nowhere-bound
the same old beaten path

I lie often
for the
same reasons
Specifically the wrong ones

I often commit
the same mistakes
and fall into the same pit

As if it's what it takes
to be held again
to be hurt, to be cherished again

I'd like to try and console myself
You point at me
just so you don't have to look at yourself

TELEVISION

Watch the news,
flip off the static box with sighs of a lifetime
Nothing new, same old, same old,
everything that we don't want to expect
happens

Maybe we'll learn to expect it more
but will the Happening and Becoming get less?
Probably not, my friend,
probably we suck

We say we learn from history
but mostly rely on luck

Some theorise there is heaven after this hell on earth
you know, you can choose to believe that if it eases your mind
We'll find something else to believe if it doesn't

THE WOLF

In the corner of my room sits a wolf that's crying
His limbs are spread loosely on my grey wing chair
and his fur looks spiky in the shadows
I know he wails a little louder when I close my eyes
He doesn't let me sleep when he waits for me to look
Not sure where he came from in the first place
I'm guessing growing a few inches taller was all it took

Maybe he also just wanted someone, alone, to befriend

Sometimes I get the feeling he is waiting
for me to reach out but I'm cold and he's sitting
too far from the bed
If it wasn't for his senses I would just
be playing dead
I turn to face him often and he's visibly upset
and I just sit there watching him shake his head instead

We never have good days, him and I
We look at each other, but never eye to eye

Most of the times he is yelling, scratching the walls,
tearing on my sheets, till I receive the message of his calls
Attention, please.

There you go, I offer it to him,
I say, here have it. Take it and leave
But he looks at me like I'm weird

So maybe I don't know how to give it to him
the way he needs it

I can't just ask him what he needs when he doesn't speak

He follows me when I go out but no one else sees
Not when we stroll down alleys and meet friends to eat
No matter how far he strays sometimes
from across the streets we'll meet

RETURNING

If it's not the chemicals
then it's something else
scrambling the ins and outs of my
brain with its scattered mind
(though most of the time it sings duets with my chest more than
my head, ripping sheet music into shreds)

It feels as though something is feeding
off the thoughts
I catch to torture myself

There are times I haven't got anything to say
and yet I feel like yelling

Other times all I want to do is go home
even when I don't know where that is

THE HEART ALWAYS CHANGES

Maybe his heart will go on to rotate around me
Maybe it'll embrace me less
Maybe it'll spit me out like a bitter aftertaste

I always fear too much
and I fear that I fear too little

OH DEAR HEART

Oh dear heart, save yourself
Will you not sing yourself to sleep
humming wishes you thought you wouldn't make

Will you not step into territory
you know you should avoid

Will you not believe words over actions
because you want to trust in pretty little lies

2 A M

I wouldn't be so scared of the dark
Weren't it for the monsters drawing their claws
up and down my neck
as my eyes close to the beat of oblivion

I've stopped wondering
what would be coming next
Stopped anticipating

What if, what if,
what if?

Just can't see a point in getting upset
What, now, at two at night
What is there to do?
Should I do something? The night isn't over yet
Perhaps fret

I wouldn't be such a bad sleeper
Wish my head was a secret keeper and leave me alone
Mind its own business
Hide the ugly thoughts even from me

Weren't it for the monsters whispering their opinions
into one ear through the other and back
Can't stand that when I wake from the rain and my head's
floating in pitch black

It won't be 2AM forever
And tomorrow will come
I'll shut it down tomorrow
For now I'll succumb

STAGE FRIGHT

You come out of your shell on stage as
if you're a butterfly spreading wings, birds
soaring high, and you only feel this way
because you get to be someone else

I will show you exactly what it feels like
to drown when you're not underwater
To fly with two feet tied to the ground
To smile with no memory of how to
and to lie and get away with it
because it's just what other people want to see
and it only ever matters which part of the story they believe

BOOKS LEFT IN THE SHELF

Wanna write a book
but can't remember the last thing I ate yesterday
Wanna watch all the series but can't
keep my mood consistent
Wanna make a movie but can't
remember to drink water

Help me guitarist with big brown eyes
Wake me gentle blonde ice queen
where can I find meaning to the life I'm living
and when did we decide we needed to have one?

Help me know what I'm supposed to do with it
Touch me blue veins, strong chest, soft touch
What am I supposed to do with it
without it
Forget it ? Like books left in the shelf
When will I read them and what happens if I never do?

MIRRORS

We can't escape
no matter how many times we walk past the mirror
to avoid looking at ourselves

We can't escape the questions we ask
and the mind needs the bitter tasting bits
to get stronger

ALL THE TIME

I love the way I write me up
and pin me down
I do it all the time
the sudden overthinking
the downward spiral in
moments that could've been happy

I love the way I cross me out
I'd rather do it myself than have someone else do it
(Sometimes I can't differentiate it)
Is this what we call "thinking our way out of happiness"?

I love the way I feel so wrong
I do it all the time
I don't let myself be happy for too long
or else I'm committing a nefarious crime
and I don't feel real

I don't need it nor do I want it
I'd like to think I don't need the protection
before anything even takes place
but I do it all the time

I love the way I could be okay
if I wasn't doing this all the time

LOVELY

This is a lovely life and it's not supposed to be this way
I watch movies 'cause I hope I'll be in them one day
Can you go home once without going to die?

I want to be so lovely
Tear the skin from my bones
Be whittled down to nothing
until I'm small enough

I can't stand the silence when it swallows me up
I don't think it's ever spat me out again
It's the modern nightmare

Dry me out like a bouquet and let my petals
fall lazily, elegantly
Hang me decoratively throughout the apartment,
brittle and thin and lifeless and lovely

HISTORY OF US

HAND-ME-DOWNS

We lost ourselves in hand-me-downs
and they concluded we were fraud
At first we knew we had problems
but it was more than being humanly flawed
I sat staring at the open door for an entire Summer

A letter being written, only years too late
Same dinner table, same people,
same stupid old mistakes
Different circumstance
Couldn't even call this a date
Cause this time it's not fate

I THINK I MIGHT KNOW WHY

I know what I look like to you
Am I being unreasonable because I speak up
when my blood freezes upon your words or
is it, perhaps, because you'd rather have it easy?
Quiet, you want me
Uncomplicated, that's how you need it
Or else it isn't love, is it?

You ask why I act like I'm crazy
(Maybe because I am)
My flesh and blood and father
(That's what I thought until that one day)
abandoned me when I was laughing about
sand stuck between my toes
(I realised you two were a thing
and I was nothing)
on our family holiday
(You'd rather call me
nuts, overly jealous)
Upped and left when I was thirteen
(Than admitting to yourself)
And I couldn't think of why
(You're a wolf,
you could never be loyal)
or what I had done wrong to deserve that
(I hope one day she realises
The way you've done it to me)
or what about me seemed so useless
(You're bound to do the same thing to her)

I've wondered the same thing all my life
Re-lived it each year on my birthday
twenty-third of November

On his birthday
twenty-sixth of December

Get reminded when Ma's face falters
just a tiny bit
You and him, the same, make me wonder if
anyone will ever think this girl is worth it

You ask why I act crazy
I think I might know why

SAND BODY

It's no use pretending
that they're in love with you too
when all they do
is to contradict their tongue
as you lilt on it

It's no use staying in place
when you're the one soaked
in somebody else's mistake

You're a sand body and your time is running

PHOTOGRAPHS

On the wall previously hung proof of afternoons
where things were good between you, me and the moon
as you embraced me
And we were happy, it happened, you did love me

On the wall previously hung a row of photographs
taken on dreamy days of the past, by you and me and us,
stupid blurred photographs of skin to skin and toe to toe, of me
and another human being being human, being naked to the core
because we know each other way too well or not quite enough

Now outside that photograph your gaze is
a little intense, a little desperate,
I hang my head down low and in this moment
I think we thought the same thing;
that maybe, sometimes, things are already too far down
to be mended again

I took them off, those photographs, like stories from the past
There's no reason to put them up again

SEESAW

You dug me into the sand as I happily
cheered you on until I was gone
I was trusting you to dig me back out
I was trusting you'd dig me back out

I can't help but think
maybe you thought you were the only one hurting
maybe you wanted so badly for me to be hurting too

Without knowing,
you turned into a person I never thought you
were capable of being

and as long as you weren't hurting just
as much as me
you weren't sorry

EVERGREEN HOUSE

I opened every curtain wide
and tilted every window
and the doors were slammed open
as if it helped me catch a scent of you somehow,
as if it helped me stop you in your tracks

My chest felt like baby birds were tugging on it, scooping out
part of a soul,
my heart almost burst from racing so badly
and my eyes were blocked from all the aching or was it just the
dreaming
or the running?

I wasn't devastated about you being gone
and I still missed you,
just in a different way
In the evergreen house that was once ours
even that went away

MUDDY LIAR

What meant more to you?
The way my face lit up when I saw you
or how hard I cried when you let go?

I feel like I knew how to miss you at some point
but none of it feels real
It's all a lie I've made up, a false interpretation of a verse
that I put on my tongue on my own

It's not that you're a fraud, it's that my outlook was flawed,
and you wore a crown in all the wrong places

What does your picture of me look like?
You're more grounded, plausible, more rational,
your aspiration isn't playing with your own perception

You see me as I am and I saw you as you weren't
When the sound of your warm breath was not enough
to fill the emptiness in our conversation, I knew it was damp

If I wasn't smart enough to know I was the one mistaken,
I'd call you a liar
The two of us be damned

LACK OF

The story of Lack Of
begins with a tune of Love,
like many of the poems above
I love too much, too much, too much
Maybe it's because I've had
too little, too little, too little

Maybe it's time to grab a drink,
another truth to digest and put to rest, don't you think?
Debunk, or you'll let life do its thing
Either way you're drunk and there's always new questionable
ballads to sing

And there you stand, and you take it
(Is there even anything to give?)

The problem with a person with a lack of love is,
I guess, growing up they had no idea what it
looks like and whether there's a wrong or right kind
They swallow artistry for a taste,
compare movies to a face,
have pipe dreams on replay

They write libretto that looks a little like reality,
Something most could never be,
Make up a line that's a little less painful,
So much so their stories turn sort of wasteful,
and their eyes keep missing out
on what love is truly about

They can believe what is there
and so easily see what isn't

TRANSITION

Play your tune for reminders of nights
Eat up all the memories
Dart in races in your mind
Let it take you to the edge of oblivion

Listening to you serenade felt like holding seashells
to your ear, breathing deeply, sinking in
Translating,
"You'll make it to the other side,
but it's never going to be with me"

Shards of glass bearing gifts of the past
Wearing costumes of bloody regret

Left with the Quiet you'd orchestrated,
the piece you wrote somewhere in the attic
of my mind
That piece you wrote on finding each other,
desensitising, worshipping Aphrodisia someplace else

Crescendo,
there will be more cassettes to last
you a lifetime
of unpredictable delights

WHEN THE PARTY'S OVER

Tell me, have we met before?
I can't decide from the hesitant curve
formed by your lips and the redness
your eyes display when the lights fondle
your iris.

Have you seen me before?

It feels as if you had, from the way you know
about my nervous tapping of my fingers
on the edge of this sofa.

It feels like a deja-vu, a seen-before, a felt-before,
so have I seen you before?

It feels as if I had, from the way your hand
feels familiar upon the slightest touch.
You seem like you have somewhere to run,
I get startled by the way it pains me a little.

You get up when we're done, I stay down.
The party's over and so is your frown.
We decide to stare at a brick wall.

If i stay, would you scoot closer?
If you stay, would I slow down?
The answer is no so I know it is over
No, I don't think I should be here any longer
No, I don't think we've met before

OVER IT

I thought I was over it
I thought I'd have it under control

But healing is the thing that comes in waves, isn't it
And it's okay to hurt all over again when it washes over me

There's simply no timeline for regret
or trying to forget
when all you're trying to do is heal
and the healing is a mess
But it is still a process
A game of chess for blessing

Setting you free was like watching the sun
falling into the sea to remark we are done

C'EST VRAI

C'est vrai
I've loved you for me
I've loved what was broken in you
It just felt so goddamn familiar
Thinking it would somehow fix me
or trick me into feeling OK

C'est vrai
I don't think we were right after all
even if it felt so wrong to be apart
To love something broken
that was out to break me
was never the plan
And it was never going to
heal either of us

C'est vrai
Tu n'es pas mon amour
Not anymore

SHOULDN'T BE MAD

When I saw your face darken to the sight of
me kissing him on the staircase, I wasn't happy
you were hurt. I wasn't happy I found love and
that yours was foul. I wasn't happy this was how
things would turn out. I was just happy to know
that, back then, when all I did was cry over you,
I shouldn't have been mad at you for healing
and trying to be happy. You shouldn't be mad,
too.

STRAY CAT

They said if you feed her
she'll come back like a stray cat
She'll never forget the route to your venue
and the way you made her heart full

ARE YOU IN LOVE?

HAZE

Drunken nights in a yellow summer's haze
but vodka makes me sick
We've been dreaming here for days
Waiting for that change to kick,
A hook to flick,
Or reality to click
into place

Oh, it is you that I want in this bed
In your arms my faith is blind
So please, replace them in my memory
Hold me when I whisper to be kind

LACE STRING

I don't think it's fair
Having your sleeves up
With that hardly resistible grin of yours
Or the glance of fiery assurance
Or the gentle brush across the back of my hand

You're tracing silver lines
On dangerous ground there,
Honey,
You're getting the taste
Of a sun-kissed lifetime

YOU HATE THE COLD

You hate the cold but you step on your
balcony with bare feet and your pyjamas
to watch a concert of the birds singing
morning symphonies

You know the chords on your guitar to that song
you adore by heart from the movie that made you cry
and you play them to me like a poem

My breath forming clouds in winter air is
evidence of the flames burning in my stomach
and the ashes sticking to my lashes

You whisper my name against my lips like a prayer
to the gods we don't believe
Ever since you've touched me it feels like coming home
Warm as the morning sun filtering through the window
The light of a blanket of stars dances between my fingers
You hate the cold but you keep smiling at the simple
beauty of the northern night sky

PHOTOGRAPHS OF YOU

I take photographs of you as though it's the
only way to keep you close when you're away
The moment the sky turns a clear blue or when
there are specks of pink and orange in the later
hours of the day, I am bound to think of you
I don't need reminders but I'll still take
photographs of you
I think I am in love and it's tough to say
I know this because I've never felt this way
and yet I know this feeling feels this way
I don't need proof but I see it on these photographs anyway

ROSY CHEEKS

Welcome to the final show,
where I take hesitant steps towards you
with ears gone hot
and cheeks painted peach
and I think even mother hasn't seen my
face get warm colour in a very long time
and I think even my friends would notice
how my drawing has altered from
black and white
to splashes of brightest yellow
of hope and nothing but hope

Maybe also a tint of fear
but that's what it means
to approach someone with rosy cheeks

I DON'T KNOW IF I'M ALLOWED TO FEEL THIS WAY

I can't easily open up to you
even if I wanted to
You see,
I'm scared because I don't know
what you'll mean to me
in a week or two

Underlying, waiting for that catch
Even a fool like me must know that

It's easy to get insecure when you meet someone
too great to be true
And these things I'm feeling in my chest,
do they feel infinite to you?

They scare me, they won't stop giving births in my chest
They reach the ceiling of stars

I want to slow down, savour every moment
leading up to the moment our longing lips touch
It's so hard to hold back, the hunger of souls
We say goodbye to meet again

We're so good together that it's bad
I can't look away from you when you
attempt to resist me
We both know where it ends

YOU SMELL OF LOVE NOW

We didn't slowly burn and build
We ran and tumbled,
right into each other,
no warning
We didn't even stop each other

I love how we sound together
Your crackle of laughter
up the chimes of my spine
and the hush hush hush
of the calmer mind of mine

You smell of love now,
taste of trust now,
When you leave the house a bit early
and your cheeks are red from the tint
little smiles leave on your skin.

Thank him and thank yourself
for putting your story on that shelf
For loving you fully, when your taste
was braised of previous heartache

And the flowers he gives you
are taking root in you

The smallest thing can wreck a ship on the sea
And you, body of waves I long for
Right here, as always, by the shore
The sea in the painting look like a thin line
I look at you like the blueprint of the sun
coming up on the horizon
each day
You look at me like you're afraid
of sinking and slipping away
The footprints and the dunes
Washed up perfume, deep scents on your chest
And the storm riots in your eyes
Your hair flows like the current itself
I'm the shore and will always long for you
I'll always have love for the sea

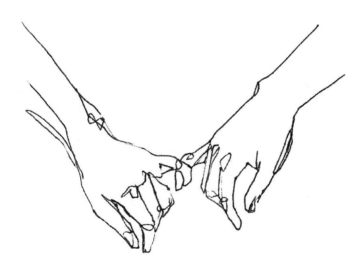

HURRICANE

I've wanted to kiss you all evening
and when I finally did
the world began to spin
in a deadly beautiful way

I'd love to feel it again
and again
and I don't care if it'll mean a hurricane

She, as a writer, was not always liked back
The way she had dreamed in her poems
Little did they know,
they couldn't limit the rain
and she was always a hurricane

SUMMER DAY

You weren't as easy to find as it was to lose 'em
but easier to touch and even easier to love,
our limbs and minds softly intertwined
on that hazy Summer day

I was waiting by the pier, I knew you would come to me
Only didn't expect you where you turned up to be

I hummed songs of
It's okay,
some day I am going to be with you,
we'll be sitting on the dock of the bay,
singing lyrics we never thought we knew

IN THE BEDROOM

Please wake me in the morning
So I can see your face in the peachy dawn
through my bedroom's open window
So I can kiss your palm in mine
flick you around my finger tip
claim your bottom lip
love you in the daylight

SIT

Sit near me just to be,
all the while we don't speak a word
I glance away from you sometimes to catch my breath

Hard to admit I've thought about you today
long before you even came
and I will probably resume when you're home

Look at me while we still have time
Hold my hand till after prime
Come listen to my every rhyme
and let's never end this song

You're a child of sun since you're the one who brings it to me
Keep me warm, just for a little while longer
Stay by my side so these mountains are hardly hills
Make sure you keep in mind, I love you,
even the parts that have to go home

STILL STANDING

You and I,
we've been scared of love
and what it did to us

The only thing I know is this

I'm full of wounds
and still standing on my feet

Up until this moment
we're always looking at each other
like we're about to kiss
That's the whole beauty of this

We're lovers standing with fingers
intertwined, your legs caught with
mine, your fingers stick just like
honey on my skin

You are still standing, you could have
chosen anyone but me but the way
the moons and the sun phases work,
I think it's meant to be
We're meant to be standing, still

HOME

I'll be home soon and
I like my name in your mouth
Does it feels like love dripping from your
lips when you say it? Because that's how I
catch it, and
I want you with me, even when I'd rather be
alone and the little things we do have become
the big ones

I wish it will always be like this
That I'll never leave this home

I'd hate for the sheets on our beds to shift
To wake up one morning with the half-moon
still lingering over our windows, and realise
that I'll have to go, or you'll have to go
and we have to leave each other behind
and we feel like we no longer belong together

A time might come when what I call my home
will not longer be mine
I wish it will never end this way
That I'll never leave this home

WHAT IS COMING

It's too late to go home so just stay
I promise I'll be your happiness one day
We've both lost before
It doesn't mean we're set up to fail

Stories are hard to change
Truths hard to bend
We'll remember the days of other things we've done
And that we once belonged to another
What is coming is better than what is gone
And when we realise this we'll be chasing the sun

OCEAN LOVER

Our love could have been a child of the ocean
Just like tides, you pull me in, no matter if I've
been a good or bad person
Your dedication, your loyalty,
your late night calls to say Goodnight
remind me of a soft, glistening Blue that
artists like Eugène Boudin dreamt of and
often made use of in their lifetime
You're a painting of mine, let me have this.
Your touch is passionate, calming,
like the crash of waves dancing
during a sunset on my feet
They take a journey with me.
We're following the glistening tides
and shimmering blue waves,
so safe, so reassuring.
I wake up and I'm salt water and
my veins are a little blurry
I can pick you up when the wind is blowing,
I can stretch my hands to your size until they fit
only so we can drift (together, never apart)
I think that's the thing with you and me,
our story is the sun sparkling in the sea

THE WAY YOU CAN LOVE

Your presence is
my favourite sensation of
petrichor warmth,

Your touch
feels like an extension
of mine,

Your smile
is as pure
as that of a child

You astonish me in the way you can love
I wish one day we can both love completely,
silly, out of bounds, out of sense
You don't have to play pretend
since you've already noticed all of it
the quirky and the ugly parts no one else really gets to see
And you love me regardless
Even the man who was supposed to love me
most left his baby behind
And you love me regardless

WE LIE HERE

Fine line between sheets
your apple and my peach
in our picnic basket of worries
a thunderstorm with thoughts
and yet we sit on beaches
count sand stones of all sorts

Why am I always so scared of being left
when I can think of all the reasons
of why I'm never leaving you
And why can't I believe you have
reasons to stay, too?

WE'RE FINE I THINK

I peek a glance at you from the other end of the bed. We're fine I think. Think maybe loving is easy but everything else isn't so when everything else doesn't fall into place, love becomes hard, too. Not always. But there are hard times. Not always. But there are battles. Not always. But there is resentment. Loving makes the future scary. I'll look at you because I don't know what will happen. I'll look at you for the time I have left with you.

Because even if we stay together in a world without an end and our love is the most constant thing we can be sure of, if everything else doesn't fall into place we won't know what will survive. You feel like liquid sunrise, my demons are singing praises, and you must be an angel in disguise.

I AM LOVE

I wrote so much, over and over again,
about how other people made me feel or
the many ways I felt about them
That I only realised after your fingers intertwined
with mine, you were the first to write about me,
leaving love poems on my skin with your lips

I am now someone who makes you feel good
Someone worth thinking about during the day
Someone causing a smile
I will never forget the way holding you makes me feel
Like I embody love
Like I have it bottled up inside me
and it's ready to burst because there's just so much of it
Like I am made of nothing but it
Like I am it
Like I am love

DAY AFTER DAY

Good night my lover, my dear,
It's hard for me to leave you be
Stuck on daily fantasy
But it will get to me eventually
I'm trying to see the real side of it,
of us,
The side that isn't driven by fear nor lust,
Instead the side I know is so lovely, pretty

Good night my lover,
I will lie down to sleep now
for the safest thought that I have is you
For bearing with me I can only thank you
Day after day
As does our love grow
Day after day
I am sorry
It takes me day by day
I am sorry
but I will get there

WATCHING SUNSETS BY YOURSELF

BARS IN BERLIN

It's funny cause the less you think
and talk about something, the less
it'll be a real problem to you.
The moment you indulge in your fear,
no matter how ridiculous and unrealistic,
it'll tear at you. Don't let it.
Say it with me. You don't need anyone.
Once you realise that, you're no longer
codependent. You're free and nothing can
hurt you.

When I forget to remember there was
good stuff too, I want to forget to remember
all the bad

TELESCOPE

In the end I don't know where or what I am
Nor do I really care to know
I just live to heal the hurt I see

SERENDIPITY

Means finding pleasure
on accident
She was that, in a bottle
She was the fire in a jar
without a lid
She was the garden in the
breeze of the night
and the moonlight bleaching
clouds
She was your favourite mishap

SOFTER BLUE

They said someday this hurt will be useful
The churning surges of the bile, the fright
will collapse against the shore that night,
the coastline you've been avoiding,
desperately wishing it ceased to exist
just when your entire world is made of it
and the sea is the only way to go

Tell me at some point I will become one with it,
where I won't scarper, won't cover,
will put the past behind, the hurt aside

Tell me a balmy sunset lies ahead
as I rest with the tide and play with the waves,
they'll carry me, sweet child of sun,
and my heart will be of steel,
of solid fire, soft blue cushion,
and parts of it will fight,
that's alright
It's always time to heal

ATTACHMENT STYLE

Happiness has no limbs to be attached
It's our fault we make love a thing that's
supposed to catch us at all times until
it snap at us

We forget love is a person
and that person can't carry all
two weights

People are people and we can't
make them out to be more than
they are; they're already trying
their best

THE LIGHTHOUSE

The light's on but nobody's home
It's the end of the world out there
I think we've lost each other at the beach,
somewhere between wet clumps of sand
and tousled sheets
When life rolls on, will you be there?
If i get on a place, will you be sleeping
somewhere?
Standing on a ledge, scared to take the leap
There's not a night when I stop counting sheep,
running, hiding, stopping, flighting,
hitting, kicking, downward spiralling

Are you sure you've passed the tunnel?
Are you sure I'm doing this right?

We talked about the shore a dozen times,
where there's struggle not worth the fight
This road is long without you

I'm still wondering whether we will seek to reach it
See it, climb it, sit on it,
poke it, poke it, that lonely little place
at the shore

IHYK

Some days are meant to be yesterday
I hope you know
You are loved no matter how you feel
I hope you know
No matter where you are
you've got permission for it
You can feel what you feel but
you gotta let go,
I really hope you know

CHARACTER DEVELOPMENT

I'm starting to like myself more and more
every time I'm petrified,
I don't think
or I end up disappointed,
every time I give it a pinch
and take a sip of the Unknown
and swallow it whole
even if it turns sour

YOU KNOW THIS

It's okay that you're happy
and then suddenly you're not
It's okay you're angry
and feel wounded in certain spots
where the light of day never hits

It's okay this is not what you want
or if it takes a while to accept it
It's okay you're disappointed
because not every shoe fits

It's okay to feel this way
and then not

This is not permanent, you know this,
you know this, how come not believe it?

The fleeting thing in your chest doesn't define who you are
You know this,
yet you forget this

A LITTLE KINDER

I have seen all the things in the world
that I love
in you
You are your the daylight of the candle
I've watched you laugh,
I don't know why it escapes your memory
You're braver than you think
and you're doing most to get better
so you can be a little kinder
and believe in you a little louder
As loud as you can
from the bottom of your heart
to the top of your lungs

STILL WATERS

It's fine,
I'm still waiting to live
and looking to love
but it's fine
It could be that not everything will set into place
Hell, I'm sure something will always not make
sense to me
But cheers to life because
we'll travel and meet people
we'll drive through cloudbursts and
rainbows and the fall of leaves from orange trees
and I'll cry because it's beautiful
That black pit of my head will probably be there,
still,
but I don't have to feed it

LOVE LANGUAGE

How have you been lately?
Please be careful on your way home,
you can always let me know if
you need anything, really anything
at all
I am proud of you even
when you're not
or it seems no one else is
noticing
You are doing so well
Trust me when you can't see it
yourself
I hope you get some sleep now, love,
I hope you get good rest
even in another time I know
you try your best

FRESH SHEET

Picture yourself in aged lurid days
sitting on a stool, ad libitum purchased,
will you look back, saying "don't!"
or will you nod and tell the child
"What are you waiting for? Go!"

Perhaps you won't give anything away at all?

You'll know not every curtain drawn
acts as one eternal dawn, fear
That you won't wake up to
experience an alternative to
what you've learned and grown
accustomed to
Fear not that things will change
Memories will be lost and a few
people will come

You don't have to die to bloom

while obstacles anew
and fade when you are done

JOURNEY

For a long time in summer I doubted I would
find love that didn't hurt. I did not know where
I stood, whether I wanted to stand there.
Watch, observe. I heard horror stories.
I had enough spare keys to give away, that's not
the issue. My house is strongly built, I know
because I did. Hopefully I won't lose some shelfs
and trip over some stairs in the hallway. Have
my books taken away from me. Have my paintings
smudged for eternity.
For a long time I believed my past. I believed what
my past has taught me, what it has robbed me of.
It dug holes into my walls, swiped away neatly
picked furniture and shattered my mirror
in the bedroom.
I didn't know any better when the past
would be the teacher. How am I supposed to
know any better?
How can a little girl simply know any better?
I did not save myself over the years, growing up
living just an ordinary life. I don't think anyone
can really be saved, and if you can't seem to
save yourself, I doubt someone else outside your skin
would be able to. But somehow you expect it and
you turn miserable. Because you're tired. PLEASE,
change, please come, please get me out of here and
get on the phone with me, wherever that is, I can't
do this by myself.
I aimlessly stride along as I look up at the sky
and keep my head up ignoring the shadows behind
the trees lurking. Sometimes they would brush
may flowers to attack me and I would trip over,
startled to death. Crying, yelling into the void, at myself.

But never
a step
back.

It is not in other hands to feel for your torn skin,
rub the sensitive part of your shoulder to make
you feel safe and sound
It is not the strangers' kiss that holds the answers
We live to look for them alone
We look for them to live
The answers never come though,
just shoes to limp feet that fit

I have seen it coming.
I have felt me drowning,
slowly, and then all at once,
I don't like it here, you know
It's different,
maybe I knew it was gonna be

NOT ALLOWED TO THINK THAT

She's so pretty, too pretty
Much much prettier than I could ever be
Look at her nose, mine is too wide. I wish it was as cute as hers.
She can wear those shorts because her legs
aren't crazed by stretch marks, like mine are
If I post things like her,
if I look a little like her,
if I write captions the way she does,
will I get people to like me the way they like her?
I mean *look at her*
I feel like a six out of ten, with her smile brightly,
so fulfilled and happy and perfect
I am far from that
How do you get there? And what does it take?
I'd like to know

No, stop.
You're not allowed to think that.
How dare you trust a kodak moment of pixels on a screen?
How dare you consume negativity towards yourself?
How dare you think of becoming a carbon copy?
You think you're too damp for a spark
but you view yourself selectively.
No, you're not allowed to think that.

IMPATIENCE

They say give it some time
If things are supposed to happen,
they will
If you mean enough to people,
they will come find you again
If they truly love you,
they will forget
but they also say villains don't
get happy endings
but it is nowhere to be said
that villains should give up

STREETLIGHTS

A face full of exhaustion,
a mind full of peace,
I've found my inner coach taking over again.

Under the streetlights
I found what I've been looking for
Not quite an object,
not quite a person
It was an answer that I had no questions for.

Street lights and open oceans,
quite the same to me
If you plan to find yourself
meet me where your eyes leer
Between the shadows and light,
stands the might that is your mind

You're stronger than you think
You say you're drowning, but
Look! your head is afloat.
Live through the engulfing monster
Do not forget the feeling of cool air in the back of your throat

Don't expect the Moon to sing for you
Don't expect the Stars to shine
They only come to listen
Do you have the time?

HAVEN'T SEEN IT COMING

I have seen it coming
I have seen me losing myself,
piece by piece, word by word
I have been trying to reach the bright smoke
of expectations that hovers around my head
I don't like it here

I have seen it coming
I have seen those good grades fade
I have seen me dead
I don't like it here

I haven't seen it coming
but I am still here
I'm not feeling that way anymore
I barely remember how it feels
I haven't seen it coming
but I am happy here

HAPPY

If I could crawl I'd take my time
If I could walk I'd meet you half-way
and meet you there
If I were gone would you think
my name? And if I was there would
it be the same?

We've got to learn that we are ok
or at least we will be
when they leave

IMPECCABLE

Blemishes, defect, weakness
Everyone thinks they have it
and that they shouldn't
Everyone wastes time
trying to cover up what we're not
and painting facades onto us
that we want to be
and concealing what we truly are

Society has made it more than clear
that being ourselves isn't enough
and yes, they'll tell you to keep being you
but they'll also stomp on your dirty mattress
the moment you reveal your intimate bed
and once you let yourself be damned
by the voices that don't know better
They'll call it perfect

IMAGINE

I'm trying to imagine how it feels
to be small and feel as small
and how it feels to struggle alone,
avoiding truth to feel less lonely,
because one false friend was better
than having none at all

I'm trying to imagine how it feels
to have my heart beating out of my chest
and trying to suppress it in embarrassment

I'm trying to imagine how it feels
to have been betrayed by sweet creatures
and letting them go when I wanted them to stay

And how did it start, the new gaze in the mirror?
Where did the old one go?

Oh dear, I've found the girl once so lost she didn't know
which way to walk upon so she didn't take on any

I've found her and picked her up
by the side of the road and her eyes twinkled
like they only now awakened,
like they only now started to live

I've found her
and she's
never going back

POETS

We poets have a desperation to write
what keeps us hanging onto life
We write prose in the Winter air even
if it gets frozen

We poets will be buried in the dirt,
along with their our bones, beneath
sleet headstones of inscriptions meant
for the passerby – and our stories will be loved

We share a bond, we poets,
we come up with songs without the melodies,
we capture untold stories that peep through
the peals of laughter between drinks
We miss each other and write letters about it
We write a lot about the distance
The distance feels really unread between us
for our words will stamp the papers
and they will live now and forever

BLUEBIRD

Somewhere someone is singing across oceans
causing this deluge
Something bad has happened but don't worry,
it seems not everything fell loose
If the rain you left behind for me to deal with
taught me anything in this life
it would be that after every shower
there would be rays of sun
so I will believe the bluebird in the sky when it sings
that all will feel okay again
eventually

STRETCH MARKS OF THE FIREPLACE

Someone back then opened a door
with a loud creak shrilling on the
wooden floor
of a childhood home with a picture frame
on the warm-smoked fireplace

Not realising they would leave scratches
with their claws on the matt finish

Cozy, tender welcome, at least to the simple eye,
to anyone looking in from the outside
But this entrance was none for a kid

Yet I was born

With stretch marks on my skin
Élan vital wearing thin
Yet I live

The voice I hauled was kind
I wore it like a wreath of daisies to the next dainty bride
I put it in their hand and then there was none of it left

I never had my voice in the right place for myself
And it gets a little unfair

And there's only a few more words to spare
in all of the letters addressed to fellow others
like we couldn't be our own sisters and brothers

Have I even met myself?

Somehow I still know exactly what to say,

with those degrading ideas about myself anyway

I sit here on hot sand with my skin ripped apart
Yet I am loved

AVIATION

You can go ahead and fly for an eternity with
your head held lofty, never bethinking
Your balked musing as the weight pulling you into sinking
Bear no malice, bury hatchets,
Dismissal from the mind
Wiping slates clean, letting bygones be
bygones, turning the other cheek
A lot of different names for a thing we dread
doing
A lot of the times forgiving is no one's strong suit
with a heart too broken too many times
It's easy to forget
that not many people like to kiss
and make up because they think forgiving
means surrendering
to the people who have hurt them
but really it doesn't

GET HOME SAFE

You left your scarf behind last time, let me grab it for you
If you weren't so busy today, I would've made dessert for two
This heart replenished itself
just so that you can enter the premise
and have a warm stay
Be safe my love, treat the roads as if you
were to caress my skin
Inhale the air as if you were to live for me
Remember to stay warm as if we were
hugging on Christmas Day,
Appreciate this moment in time
as if you were to lose me today

PAINTER

Sweep the gentle brush just this once,
whisk it in hues of defying nature, mysterious bliss
Maybe draw how you feel in saturation
when you wake up in contrast to
when you go to sleep
Crop the fluid frame in the middle of the day
Tilt your slanted shape at the end of the week
Draw what it feels like to be carefree
to be walking in sand with your bare feet
Draw your nightmares
and your daydreams of the shore
and your whimsical fantasies,
all those blue-spotted scenarios in your head
that won't happen anymore
Draw you, your true you
The you that stays awake all night
counting mistakes, grains of shame instead of sheep
The you that moves in depths of thoughts sat on a never-ending
train even in your sleep
Draw
Don't dare fix anything
For once draw messily
toward the crisp green air of Spring

ACKNOWLEDGMENTS

If it wasn't for the encouragement from my readers pushing me to pursue the craft of stringing words together, I would've never had the courage to put *Seashore* out there. Thank you.

Thank you to Ngoc Anh, who not only is my friend, but an amazing artist and believed enough in my words that she would provide her stunning illustrations before even reading any of them. Still, she managed to capture the energy of this collection perfectly.

Thank you to the baristas who made the coffee I devoured writing this book and cheering me on.

Thank you to my dear friends for listening to my words over and over and over again throughout all of my chapters.

Thank you to my mother and sister, your un-conditional love for me was what shaped me into the woman that I am today and the broken and un-broken woman who wrote this book. I'm sorry and I love you.

Thank you, Gabriel, for believing in me enough for two, the loud encouragement for everything I do and the reassuring forehead kisses. I am so lucky to have you in my life the way I do and to be in love with you but that, amongst many other things, I don't have to tell you. You already know.

Thank you to the people whom I loved, those who I love, those who left and those who stayed, those who made me cry and those whose shoulders I was allowed to cry on. If any of you happen to read these and remember, I hope that when you stargaze from your English rooftop or see a white tulip in a vase in a coffeeshop or when you hear *Que será, será* played by a busker on the street, you have fond memories of me.

ABOUT THE WRITER

Hannah Cao is a writer by night living in Dresden. Growing up with her head in the clouds and her nose rooted in a book, it comes as no surprise that she would one day write one of her own. She now lives in Dresden, working full-time before coming home to write her novels of which at least one she hopes to finish at some point before she dies. She enjoys watching movies, collecting postcards and shooting with her film camera.

Manufactured by Amazon.ca
Bolton, ON

18738618R00090